# THE
# MORMON'S MISTAKE

## Register This New Book

Benefits of Registering*

- ✓ FREE **replacements** of lost or damaged books
- ✓ FREE **audiobook** – *Pilgrim's Progress*, audiobook edition
- ✓ FREE information about new titles and other **freebies**

www.anekopress.com/new-book-registration

*See our website for requirements and limitations.

# MORMON'S MISTAKE

Short, Easy-to-Read Insight into the Unbiblical Beliefs of the Mormon Church

## H. A. IRONSIDE

We love hearing from our readers. Please contact us at www.anekopress.com/questions-comments with any questions, comments, or suggestions.

*The Mormon's Mistake*
© 2021 by Aneko Press
All rights reserved. Published 1896.
Second, revised and annotated edition 2021

No part of this book may be reproduced, stored in a retrieval system, or transmitted in any form or by any means – electronic, mechanical, photocopying, recording, or otherwise, without written permission from the publisher.

Scripture quotations from The Authorized (King James) Version. Rights in the Authorized Version in the United Kingdom are vested in the Crown. Reproduced by permission of the Crown's patentee, Cambridge University Press.

*Cover Design: Jonathan Lewis*
*Editors: Sheila Wilkinson and Jeremiah Zeiset*

Aneko Press

www.anekopress.com

Aneko Press, Life Sentence Publishing, and our logos are trademarks of

Life Sentence Publishing, Inc.
203 E. Birch Street
P.O. Box 652
Abbotsford, WI 54405

**RELIGION / Christianity / Church of Jesus Christ of Latter-day Saints**

Paperback ISBN: 978-1-62245-737-3

eBook ISBN: 978-1-62245-738-0

10  9  8  7  6  5  4  3  2  1

Available where books are sold

# CONTENTS

What is the Gospel?..................................................................1

The Mormon Gospel Stated ......................................................3

Paul's Statement of the Real Gospel ........................................9

Two Gospels Contrasted..........................................................13

Mormon Doctrine of Authority ............................................17

Notes on Mormon Doctrines.................................................21

*Other Similar Titles* ..................................................................25

# WHAT IS THE GOSPEL?

On one occasion a young man came to my door. He was dressed in the conventional, pseudo-clerical style that proclaimed to anyone acquainted with the so-called Latter-day Saints that he was a Mormon "elder" – though "younger" might be a more correct term as 1 Peter 5:5 indicates:

> *Likewise, ye younger, submit yourselves unto the elder. Yea, all of you be subject one to another, and be clothed with humility: for God resisteth the proud, and giveth grace to the humble.*

Scriptural elders were invariably men of years and experience,[1] who could care for the flock of God but

---

[1] See 1 Timothy 3:2-7 and Titus 1:5-7 that indicate *elder* and *bishop* are the same; the former word refers to the age of the man; the latter to his office. In all of this, Mormonism is in dire confusion.

were not to lord it over the people of God as they would over possessions:

> *The elders which are among you I exhort, who am also an elder, and a witness of the sufferings of Christ, and also a partaker of the glory that shall be revealed: Feed the flock of God which is among you, taking the oversight thereof, not by constraint, but willingly; not for filthy lucre, but of a ready mind; Neither as being lords over God's heritage, but being examples to the flock.*
> (1 Peter 5:1-3)

In the case mentioned, the Mormon introduced himself as a "minister of the gospel, doing missionary work among the mountain towns" of California. He stated that he would be pleased to share with me some of "the principles of the gospel." I mentioned that I was also seeking to share God's good news to poor sinners as stated in 1 Timothy 1:15: *This is a faithful saying, and worthy of all acceptation, that Christ Jesus came into the world to save sinners; of whom I am chief.* So I told him that if that was indeed his objective, I would be glad to converse with him; so I asked him to be seated.

# THE MORMON GOSPEL STATED

---

"And now, sir," I asked, "would you kindly favor us (a number were present) with a short statement of what the gospel really is?"

"Certainly," he replied. "The gospel consists of four first principles. The first is repentance; the second, faith; the third, baptism for the remission of sins by one duly qualified; and the fourth is the laying on of the hands of a man having authority, for the reception of the Holy Spirit."

"Well, suppose one has gone through all this, is he then saved?" I asked.

"Oh, of course, no one can know that in this life. If one continues to the end, he will be exalted in the kingdom." Then he proceeded to open a little Testament, with which, however, he was only slightly familiar. He pointed to some proof texts showing conclusively that the Lord and the apostles preached repentance and faith. He also showed us that Peter spoke of *baptism for the remission of sins* (Acts 2:38; carefully note the verse and its context), and in at least two instances, the apostles laid their hands on people in order for them to receive the gift of the Holy Spirit:

> *Now when the apostles which were at Jerusalem heard that Samaria had received the word of God, they sent unto them Peter and John: Who, when they were come down, prayed for them, that they might receive the Holy Ghost: (For as yet he was fallen upon none of them: only they were baptized in the name of the Lord Jesus. Then laid they their hands on them, and they received the Holy Ghost.* (Acts 8:14-17)

His second proof text was Acts 19:1-6:

> *And it came to pass, that, while Apollos was at Corinth, Paul having passed through the upper coasts came to Ephesus: and finding certain disciples, He said unto them, Have ye received the Holy Ghost since ye believed? And they said unto him, We have not so much as heard whether there be any Holy Ghost. And he said unto them, Unto what then were ye baptized? And they said, Unto John's baptism. Then said Paul, John verily*

*baptized with the baptism of repentance, saying unto the people, that they should believe on him which should come after him, that is, on Christ Jesus. When they heard this, they were baptized in the name of the Lord Jesus. And when Paul had laid his hands upon them, the Holy Ghost came on them; and they spake with tongues, and prophesied.*

He also made an effort to find a verse to prove that no one can know he is saved now, but in the light of the following verses, this was an utter absurdity:

*But God, who is rich in mercy, for his great love where with he loved us, Even when we were dead in sins, hath quickened us together with Christ, (by grace ye are saved;) And hath raised us up together, and made us sit together in heavenly placed in Christ Jesus: That in the ages to come he might shew the exceeding riches of his grace in his kindness toward us through Christ Jesus. For by grace are ye saved through faith; and that not of yourselves: it is the gift of God.* (Ephesians 2:4-8)

*Receiving the end of your faith, even the salvation of your souls.* (1 Peter 1:9)

*Who shall also confirm you unto the end,
that ye may be blameless in the day of our
Lord Jesus Christ.* (1 Corinthians 1:8)

*For we are unto God a sweet savour of
Christ, in them that are saved, and in them
that perish.* (2 Corinthians 2:15)

*Who hath saved us, and called us with an
holy calling, not according to our works, but
according to his own purpose and grace,
which was given us in Christ Jesus before
the world began.* (2 Timothy 1:9)

However, in defense of his position, he pointed to Matthew 24:13: *He that shall endure unto the end, the same shall be saved.*

As to this, one need only say that endurance certainly is a proof of reality. One who said he was saved but did not endure would thereby prove the emptiness of his profession.[2]

"I quite agree with you," I said, "as to the fact that Scripture speaks of the four points you mention; but, possibly, you did not understand my question. I asked you for a statement of the gospel. If these so-called four principles are indeed the gospel, then you have a gospel without Christ – in other words, a gospel with the gospel omitted. And if you are correct, then surely the apostle Paul, at least, labored under a most serious

---

[2] I would recommend to the reader who has difficulty here, *Fallen from Grace* by W. Barker and *The Perseverance of the Saints* by F. W. Grant.

delusion, for he gives us a clear statement of his gospel and actually says nothing of either one or other of the various points that you have mentioned. No doubt you will recall the passage?"

He did not however. He was not aware of any such direct statement on the subject. In fact, it was soon evident that, with the exception of a few verses on his favorite themes, his Bible was practically a sealed book. At my direction, he turned to the fifteenth chapter of 1 Corinthians, and I invite the reader's careful attention here.

# PAUL'S STATEMENT OF THE REAL GOSPEL

---

Beginning at the first verse of this precious and wondrous portion of Scripture, we read:

*Moreover, brethren, I declare unto you the gospel which I preached unto you, which also ye have received, and wherein ye stand; by which also ye are saved, if ye keep in memory what I preached unto you, unless ye have believed in vain. For I delivered unto you first of all that which I also received, how that Christ died for our sins according to the Scriptures* [see Isaiah 53:5-6]; *and that He was buried, and that He rose again the third day according*

*to the Scriptures: and that He was seen of
Cephas.* (1 Corinthians 15:1-5)

Here I stopped, as the rest of the passage is devoted to presenting the eyewitnesses of Christ in resurrection and therefore could hardly be considered doctrinal, though the reader will benefit by meditating on the entire portion.

"Now," I said, turning to the Mormon, "we have here a statement of the gospel – the gospel which Paul preached, and it is dangerous to preach any other, as we find from Galatians 1:8-9 that the person who does so, though it be an angel from heaven, is under a curse or devoted to judgment:

*But though we, or an angel from heaven, preach any other gospel unto you than that which we have preached unto you, let him be accursed. As we said before, so say I now again, if any man preach any other gospel unto you than that ye have received, let him be accursed.*

"I understand that you teach that your gospel was revealed to Joseph Smith by an angel. If true, that would prove nothing if it is found, upon examination, to be different from that proclaimed by the apostle to the gentiles. His gospel had been received by the Corinthians; in it they stood; by it they were saved if they were real believers. It was not, you will notice, a careful obedience to certain ordinances or a walking according to certain rules, such as you mentioned a few minutes ago that would ensure their salvation, no matter how blessed such behavior might be, if properly understood; but it according to the gospel as preached by the Apostle Paul."

# TWO GOSPELS CONTRASTED

———◦•◦———

"To begin with, I noticed that this gospel is concerning a Person and quite a different person than yours brings before us. It is *concerning the Son of God*, as Romans 1:3 tells us: *Concerning his Son Jesus Christ our Lord, which was made of the seed of David according to the flesh.* Your gospel did not have a word about Him in all its four points, whereas the subject of Paul's gospel has not a word about anyone or anything except Him. Perhaps we might say the gospel could be divided into four parts, though more properly three; but even divided into four (to agree with you as far as we can), what marked differences we find! Your four parts are all concerning the poor sinner; they might be put this way:

1. The sinner repents;

2. The sinner has faith;

3. The sinner is baptized;

4. The sinner has hands laid on him.

"Now, in contrast to this, see how the true gospel can be put:

1. Christ died;

2. Christ was buried;

3. Christ has been raised again;

4. Christ is the object for the hearts of His own.

"Surely the two gospels have nothing in common. I believe you teach that Christ died for Adam's transgression, not for ours; but you maintain that while Adamic sin is remedied by the cross, our sins as individuals must be washed away by baptism. Paul's gospel tells us that Christ died for our sins, and if that is so, and *the blood of Jesus Christ, God's Son, cleanseth us from all sin*, where does baptism apply in your understanding? (1 John 1:7). If all my sins are cleansed by His precious blood, *if they were borne in His own body on the tree* (1 Peter 2:24), how many are left to be cleansed by baptism? Assuredly none. But, alas, this is but one instance in which the false gospel of Mormonism is opposed to the precious gospel of the grace of God as revealed in the Bible.

"But allow me to go on to the second point. Christ not only died, but *was buried*, yet it was written of Him, *Thou wilt not leave My soul in hell, neither wilt Thou suffer thine Holy One to see corruption* (Acts 2:27;

Psalm 16:10). His burial declares the reality of His death and surely speaks of His being forever finished with the position He took on earth. It is the end of all the relationships in which He previously stood. Scripture tells us He is dead to the law – having paid my penalty; He is dead to sin – not His own, but mine – which He bore. And I am *buried with Him by baptism into death* (Romans 6:4); so that I am not left where Mormonism would leave me as a poor, struggling soul on earth, striving to continue to the end in order to be saved, but I am counted as one who has been buried with Him – dead to it all.

"Thus, I am brought to the third point: Christ was raised from the dead, and I am raised with Him. His place is now mine in regard to acceptance with God. *Who was delivered for our offences and raised again for our justification* (Romans 4:25). His resurrection is God's open declaration that the believer is cleared from all charge of sin, since his Substitute is released from death.

"And now the One who is *alive forevermore* (Revelation 1:18) is presented as an object for the hearts of His own. *He was seen* (1 Corinthians 15:7-8); and the same apostle exclaims *We see Jesus!* (Hebrews 2:9). Poor sinners are first led to see the utter impossibility of improving or rendering themselves more fit for God's presence. The eye of faith is then directed to the One who died, and by believing, they are *justified from all things*:

> *Be it known unto you therefore, men and*

> *brethren, that through this man is preached unto you the forgiveness of sins: And by him all that believe are justified from all things, from which ye could not be justified by the law of Moses.* (Acts 13:38-39)

"Now those poor sinners who believe also have an object for the heart, even Christ in glory:

> *But we all, with open face beholding as in a glass the glory of the Lord, are changed into the same image from glory to glory, even as by the Spirit of the Lord.* (2 Corinthians 3:18)

"How different this is from what you have presented! Here;

> 'Tis Jesus first, 'tis Jesus last,
>    'Tis Jesus all the way,
> while you are focused entirely on yourself."

# MORMON DOCTRINE OF AUTHORITY

"But now, I have another question. You spoke of men with authority to baptize and lay on hands. Where do you find that in Scripture?"

To answer, he turned to Hebrews 5:4 and read, *"And no man taketh this honor unto himself, but he that is called of God, as was Aaron."*

"What honor is referred to here?" I asked.

"The honor of the priesthood giving authority to baptize and confer the Holy Spirit."

"No," I disagreed, "the first verse contradicts this. It is not a question of the priesthood at all. As all believers now are priests, there is no special priestly class in Christianity as is clearly shown in Revelation and First Peter.

*And hath made us kings and priests
unto God and his Father; to him be glory
and dominion for ever and ever. Amen.*
(Revelation 1:6)

*Ye also, as lively stones, are built up a spiritual house, an holy priesthood, to offer up spiritual sacrifices, acceptable to God by Jesus Christ . . . But ye are a chosen generation, a royal priesthood, an holy nation, a peculiar people.* (1 Peter 2:5, 9)

"The subject in Hebrews chapter 5 is the High Priesthood and refers to the Lord Jesus Christ, called of God, as noted in verse 6. Nor is there a word about baptism or imposition of hands, but it is a question of *offering gifts and sacrifices for sins* (5:1 and 2:17) and then of helping His people in this world of trial. To apply such a Scripture to human ministry is simply *handling the word of God deceitfully* (2 Corinthians 4:2) and deserves the severest censure."

Such was, in substance, what I sought to put before the misguided young man; but, alas, so deceitful is the human heart that man would rather be occupied with *his* repentance, *his* faith, or *his anything* than with God's Christ. I found this preacher of *a different gospel, which is not another* (Galatians 1:6-7) to be of the same class as thousands in professing Christendom. The Scriptures that I brought before him carried little weight compared with "present-day revelation," despite the word of Paul in Colossians 1:25 that he was made a minister *to fully preach the word of God*. So he went on his way, trusting his fleshly religion and ignoring the gospel of God.

Before dismissing the subject, I might remind the reader that neither faith nor repentance by itself is ever presented in Scripture as the ground for salvation. The cross alone is that basis. Brought to the cross by the Spirit of God, the sinner will indeed repent; trusting the work accomplished there, the soul is saved.

Nor are repentance and faith as set forth in the Scriptures to be confused with the absurdities of Mormonism. In that wretched system, repentance is confounded with penitence and faith with credulity.

In its biblical sense, repentance is self-judgment – the acknowledgment that one is lost and guilty, righteously deserving the wrath of a holy God. Faith is trusting in Christ, whose finished work removes sins forever. It is not simply crediting the statement that God exists or that the historical Jesus was the Son of God. *If thou shalt confess with thy mouth the Lord Jesus, and believe in thine heart that God hath raised Him from the dead, thou shalt be saved; for with the heart man believeth unto righteousness, and with the mouth confession is made unto salvation* (Romans 10:9-10).

Of you, reader, I would affectionately ask, Are you making the same mistake as the "elder"? You might ridicule the poor, benighted Mormon and be amazed at the semi-heathenism taught by his church, but do you, perhaps, trust in something just as hollow, when judged by the Book of God?

Remember: penances, wrought-up repentance,

consisting in peculiar frames, feelings, and renunciations; intellectual acquiescence to the truths of the Bible, miscalled faith; baptism, whether administered by a Mormon elder or an ordained clergyman; laying on of hands, or any other human rite or divinely prescribed ceremony will avail nothing for you.

Christ, and Christ alone, is your only salvation. Discarding all else, fly, then, to Him. *Believe on the Lord Jesus Christ, and thou shalt be saved* (Acts 16:31).

# NOTES ON MORMON DOCTRINES

―――――⸺·◆·⸺―――――

In the preceding sections, it has been my aim not to expose all the devious errors of Mormonism in order to refute them but rather to endeavor to show how opposed the system is to the gospel of the glory of the blessed God, which He has revealed in His Word.

It has been suggested, however, that a brief summation of some of the more important doctrines of the sect might be helpful in serving as a warning to any who, allured by fair speeches and sophistical reasonings, are drifting towards its awful vortex.

The following statements can readily be proven to be part of the weird paganism of this dreadful quasi-religious cult by examination of the more "advanced" of their publications. Some of the doctrines are often denied by the traveling "elders," whose business it is to not alarm by making public the *depths of Satan* (Revelation 2:24) but to allure people by presenting a creed as near to orthodox Christianity as possible. Nothing could be more misleading than the statement of the "doctrines of the Church of Jesus Christ of Latter-day Saints," which is now being circulated by thousands all over the land as their Articles of Faith. This was compiled by the assumed prophet Joseph Smith in the infancy of the movement, long before "present-day revelation" had introduced many of the vagaries with which it abounds today.

The leading doctrines accepted among them today are briefly as follows:

Mormons profess to believe in the Bible but also to gain additional "light" from the *Book of Mormon*, a collection of rubbish which one only needs to scan to see its utter absurdity and incongruity with the Word of God. *The Book of Doctrine and Covenants*, purporting to be a series of revelations chiefly to Joseph Smith is also considered inspired, as is *The Pearl of Great Price*, which includes *The Book of Abraham* and other apocryphal works; while "prophets" and "apostles" abound who may at any time give forth further communications, all of equal authority with these.

Mormons are really polytheistic and believe that there are many gods, but that all (except possibly the first, though their statements are conflicting) were at one time men who gained their "exaltation" to divinity by their faithfulness in this state. It is the hope of each man to become a god eventually. Their gods are supposed to retain their human forms and functions, including sex.

It is in connection with this that gives rise to polygamy. This relationship is carried on eternally. The progeny of the gods and their numerous wives will constitute their "kingdom" in the ages to come. A woman's welfare depends on her being united to one of the faithful.

Instead of the biblical doctrine of the Trinity, they teach that there are three distinct Gods, who administer the affairs of the universe. God and Christ are said to have human bodies, parts, and passions while the Holy Spirit is omnipresent and has no body. The Holy Spirit is different, as in light or electricity, the life principle of creation.

The preceding section has outlined their teaching about salvation of the living. They also publicly proclaim salvation for the dead, to whom their kind of "gospel" is being preached and who can be saved if their friends on earth will be baptized for them. They base this practice on 1 Corinthians 15:29.

As to eschatology, they have a system of prophetic teaching that embodies an exceedingly carnal view of the millennium, ushered in by the return of Christ to regather Israel, including the ten tribes, to a Zion in America and to destroy all the enemies of "the saints." This Zion is identified with Independence, Missouri. The dead will be raised and will appear on the earth. Referring to this time in his "Voice of Warning," Parley Pratt says, "Our father Adam will sit enthroned as the

Ancient of Days." He incorrectly ascribes the words of Daniel 7:9-10 to him rather than to Christ.

They also believe a final judgment will conclude all things, but few will be eternally lost. There are three "degrees of glory": terrestrial, celestial, and telestial. All will eventually be found in one of these, except the "sons of perdition."

Such a system needs no attempt at refutation. It refutes itself. No child of God, who has at all understood the cross, could be ensnared by it. But it is because many unprepared and simple ones, anxious to be saved but ignorant of God's way, are daily being entrapped by it, that I have penned this paper.

May the Lord use it to deliver many from such *abominable idolatries*! (1 Peter 4:3).

# OTHER SIMILAR TITLES

## *JESUS CAME TO SAVE SINNERS,* BY CHARLES H. SPURGEON

This is a heart-level conversation with you, the reader. Every excuse, reason, and roadblock for not coming to Christ is examined and duly dealt with. If you think you may be too bad, or if perhaps you really are bad and you sin either openly or behind closed doors, you will discover that life in Christ is for you too. You can reject the message of salvation by faith, or you can choose to live a life of sin after professing faith in Christ, but you cannot change the truth as it is, either for yourself or for others. As such, it behooves you and your family to embrace truth, claim it for your own, and be genuinely set free for now and eternity. Come and embrace this free gift of God, and live a victorious life for Him.

*Available where books are sold.*

## *THE WAY TO GOD,*
## BY DWIGHT L. MOODY

There is life in Christ. Rich, joyous, wonderful life. It is true that the Lord disciplines those whom He loves and that we are often tempted by the world and our enemy, the devil. But if we know how to go beyond that temptation to cling to the cross of Jesus Christ and keep our eyes on our Lord, our reward both here on earth and in heaven will be 100 times better than what this world has to offer.

This book is thorough. It brings to life the love of God, examines the state of the unsaved individual's soul, and analyzes what took place on the cross for our sins. The Way to God takes an honest look at our need to repent and follow Jesus, and gives hope for unending, joyous eternity in heaven.

*Available where books are sold.*

www.ingramcontent.com/pod-product-compliance
Lightning Source LLC
Chambersburg PA
CBHW052128070526
44586CB00016B/2130